THE EASY PIANO COLLECTION

TCHAIKOVSKY

GOLD

Published by:
Chester Music Limited,
14-15 Berners Street, London W1T 3LJ, UK.

Exclusive Distributors:
Music Sales Limited,
Distribution Centre, Newmarket Road, Bury St Edmunds, Suffolk IP33 3YB, UK.
Music Sales Corporation,
257 Park Avenue South, New York, NY10010, United States of America.
Music Sales Pty Limited,
120 Rothschild Avenue, Rosebery, NSW 2018, Australia.

Order No. CH74602
ISBN 978-1-84772-819-7
This book © Copyright 2009 by Chester Music.

Unauthorised reproduction of any part of this publication by
any means including photocopying is an infringement of copyright.

Edited by Jenni Wheeler.
Arranging and engraving supplied by Camden Music.

Printed in the EU.

Your Guarantee of Quality:
As publishers, we strive to produce every book to the highest commercial standards.
The music has been freshly engraved and carefully designed to minimise
awkward page turns to make playing from it a real pleasure.
Particular care has been given to specifying acid-free, neutral-sized
paper made from pulps which have not been elemental chlorine bleached.
This pulp is from farmed sustainable forests and was produced
with special regard for the environment.
Throughout, the printing and binding have been planned to ensure a sturdy,
attractive publication which should give years of enjoyment.
If your copy fails to meet our high standards, please inform us and we will gladly replace it.
www.musicsales.com

CHESTER MUSIC
part of the Music Sales Group
London/New York/Paris/Sydney/Copenhagen/Berlin/Madrid/Tokyo

1812 Overture
(Op.49)
Page 5

Dance Of The Cygnets
(from 'Swan Lake', Op.20)
Page 8

Dance Of The Sugar Plum Fairy
(from 'The Nutcracker Suite', Op.71)
Page 11

Dance Of The Reed Flutes (Danse des Mirlitons)
(from 'The Nutcracker Suite', Op.71)
Page 12

March Of The Wooden Soldiers
(from 'Album For The Young', Op.39, No.5)
Page 16

The New Doll
(from 'Album For The Young', Op.39, No.6)
Page 18

Piano Concerto No.1 in B♭ minor
(Op.23, Opening)
Page 20

March from 'The Nutcracker Suite'
(Op.71)
Page 22

Prince Gremin's Aria
(from 'Eugene Onegin', Op.24)
Page 25

Romeo And Juliet
(Fantasy Overture)
Page 28

Scene from 'Swan Lake'
(Op.20, No.1)
Page 31

Sentimental Waltz
(from 'Six Pieces', Op.51, No.6)
Page 32

Slavonic March in B♭
(Op.31)
Page 38

The Sleeping Beauty Waltz
(Op.66, No.5)
Page 40

Symphony No.6 'Pathétique', Op.74
(1st Movement)
Page 44

Symphony No.6 'Pathétique', Op.74
(3rd Movement March)
Page 46

Symphony No.5 in E minor, Op.64
(Andante Cantabile Theme)
Page 48

Waltz from 'Serenade For Strings'
(Op.48)
Page 49

Waltz in E♭ major
(from 'Album For The Young', Op.39, No.9)
Page 54

Waltz Of The Flowers
(from 'The Nutcracker Suite', Op.71)
Page 56

Waltz from 'Swan Lake'
(Op.20, No.2)
Page 62

Pyotr Ilyich Tchaikovsky

Pyotr Ilyich Tchaikovsky was undoubtedly the greatest Russian musical talent of the Romantic era. With his gift for eloquent melody and his mastery of writing for the orchestra, he created dramatic and evocative works through which he could express something of his tortured private life.

Tchaikovsky was born in 1840, living in St. Petersburg from 1848. He showed early promise at the piano and began to compose seriously after his mother died in 1854, but he was obliged to take a job in the Ministry of Justice after he left school. However, in 1863 he entered the St. Petersburg Conservatory.

Although Tchaikovsky championed traditional Russian music and culture, his musical education at the Conservatory was entrenched in the Western Classical tradition, a legacy he passed on when he became Professor of Harmony at the Moscow Conservatory in 1866. Because of this, Tchaikovsky stood apart from his 'nationalist' contemporaries who were concerned with developing a particularly Russian style.

'The Five', as they were known, heavily criticised Tchaikovsky's *First Symphony*. However, the leader of the group, Mily Balakirev, encouraged him by suggesting he write a work based on Shakespeare's *Romeo and Juliet*. Balakirev gave Tchaikovsky a plan for the work and even wrote the first four bars. The result was the *Romeo And Juliet Fantasy Overture* (1869), which remains a popular concert piece.

The most famous work of this early period is his *Piano Concerto No.1 in B♭ minor* (1874–75). This highly dramatic work has been criticised for having a major structural 'fault', in that the famous opening theme, which is included in this album, never reappears again in the work. It was rejected by the pianist Nikolai Rubinstein as ill-composed and unplayable, although he later became a great interpreter of it.

In 1876 Tchaikovsky began a 14-year correspondence with a wealthy widow, Nadezhda von Meck. She supported him emotionally and financially on the condition that they should never meet. She became his confidante as he struggled with his homosexuality and his desire to avoid public shame. To 'cure' himself he married in July 1877. Antonina Miliukova had professed her love for him in a letter just three months earlier, and Tchaikovsky could not even remember what she looked like. The marriage was a shambles and by October the couple were permanently separated. Tchaikovsky's near-hysterical state is recorded in letters to Mme von Meck and his brother Modest, as well as being clearly apparent in his music. *Symphony No.4* is full of emotional excess and hysteria, and the opera *Eugene Onegin* has obvious parallels to his own situation, as it tells the story of a girl who is rejected by a man who fascinates her.

Tchaikovsky's flair for writing dramatic music coupled with his brilliant orchestration meant that he was perfectly suited to writing for the ballet, and his three scores are generally considered to be the culmination of the Romantic ballet tradition—*Swan Lake* (1875–76), his masterpiece *The Sleeping Beauty* (1888–89), and *The Nutcracker* (1891–92).

Although known primarily as an orchestral composer, Tchaikovsky wrote over 100 pieces for the piano. *The Seasons*, a suite of 12 piano pieces, was published throughout 1875–76 in a monthly periodical. Two years later he composed the *Album For The Young*, a set of 24 pieces with descriptive titles, which he declared to be '…in the style of Schumann'.

After a long stay in Europe, Tchaikovsky returned to Russia in 1878 and soon after he resigned from the Moscow Conservatory and lived on his allowance from Mme von Meck. The strain of trying to obtain a divorce affected his work, his wife only finally agreeing to it when she had an illegitimate child. However, during this period he wrote what was to become one of his most famous works, the *1812 Overture*. Commissioned to celebrate the 70th anniversary of Russia's victory over Napoleon in 1812, Tchaikovsky did not have much enthusiasm for the piece and declared it to be 'very loud and noisy', but it was an immediate success and its popularity has never waned.

Tchaikovsky began to recover, both emotionally and musically. The immensely popular *Symphony No.5* and *Symphony No.6* are highly emotional and dramatic. The anguished and sorrowful *Symphony No.6*, first performed on 28th October 1893, was given the title 'Pathétique' by Tchaikovsky's brother Modest. Three days after the premiere, Tchaikovsky was brought before a court of his peers from his old school. He was accused of bringing the school into disrepute through rumours of his homosexuality and was sentenced to commit suicide.

One week later, Tchaikovsky was dead. The cause of his death is shrouded in uncertainty. The official reason given was that he died from cholera as a result of drinking untreated water, but it is also possible that he killed himself by taking arsenic.

Kate Bradley

1812 Overture
(Op.49)

Composed by Pyotr Ilyich Tchaikovsky

© Copyright 2008 Dorsey Brothers Music Limited.
All Rights Reserved. International Copyright Secured.

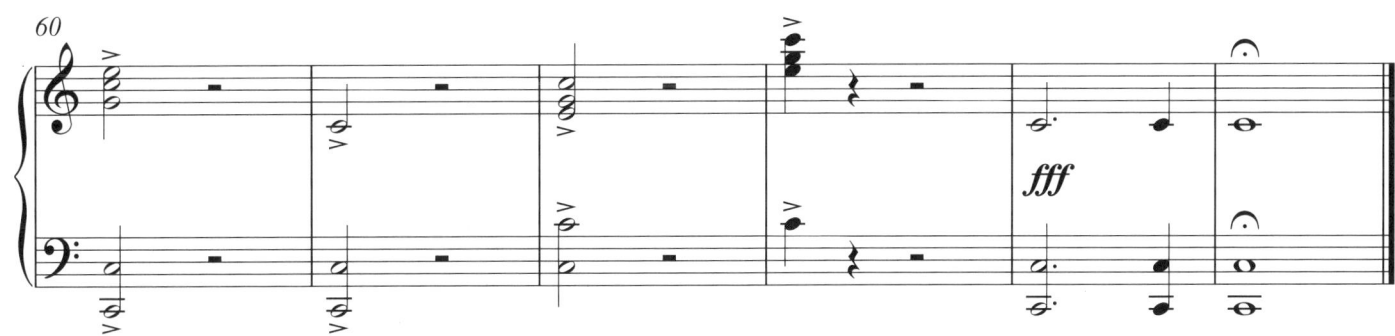

Dance Of The Cygnets
(from 'Swan Lake', Op.20)

Composed by Pyotr Ilyich Tchaikovsky

© Copyright 2008 Dorsey Brothers Music Limited.
All Rights Reserved. International Copyright Secured.

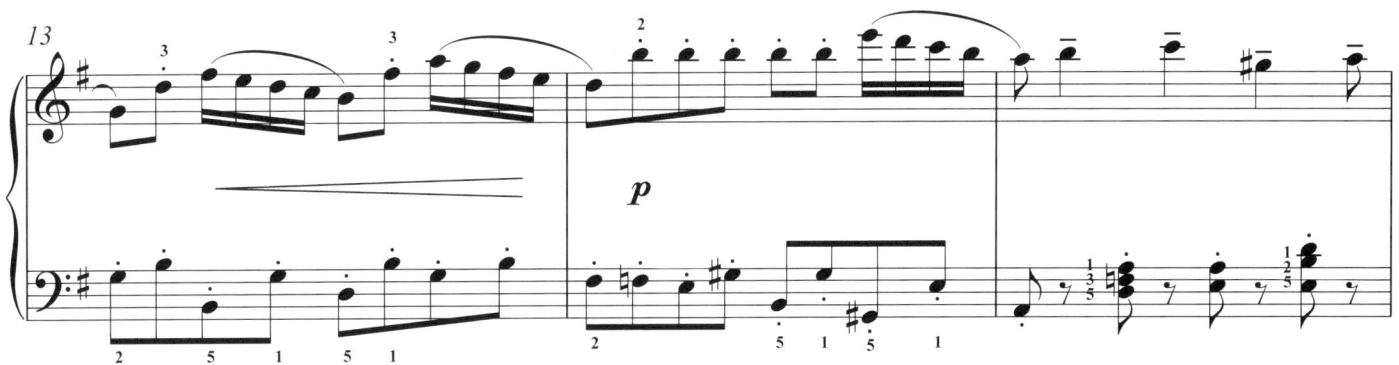
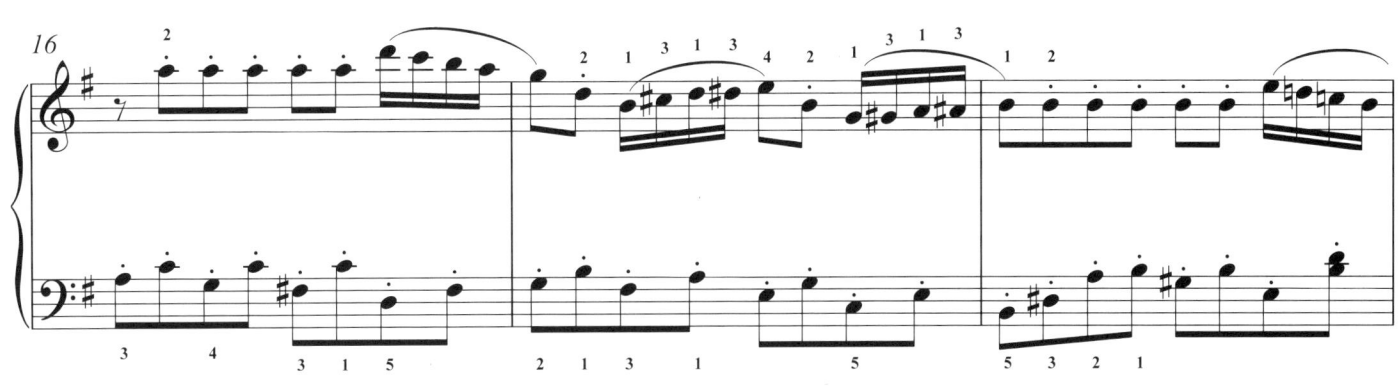
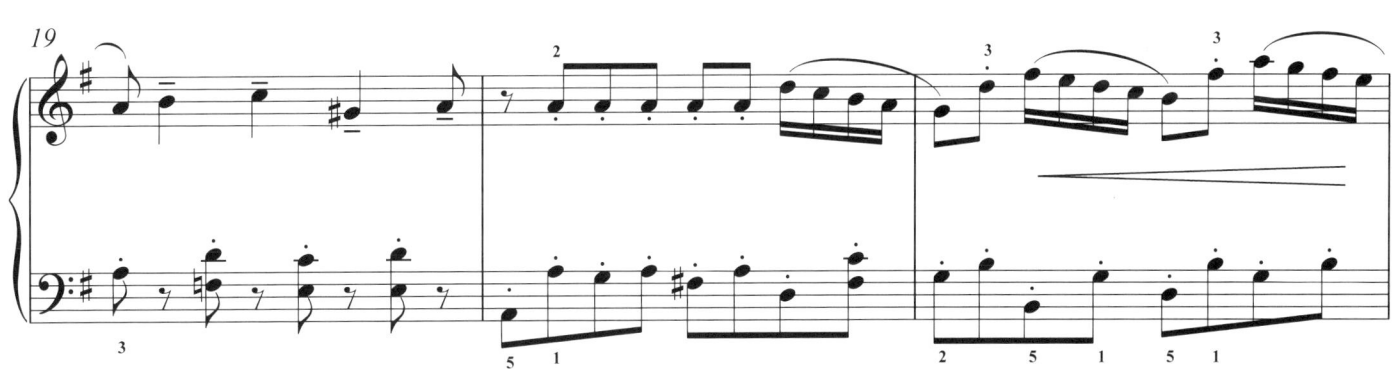

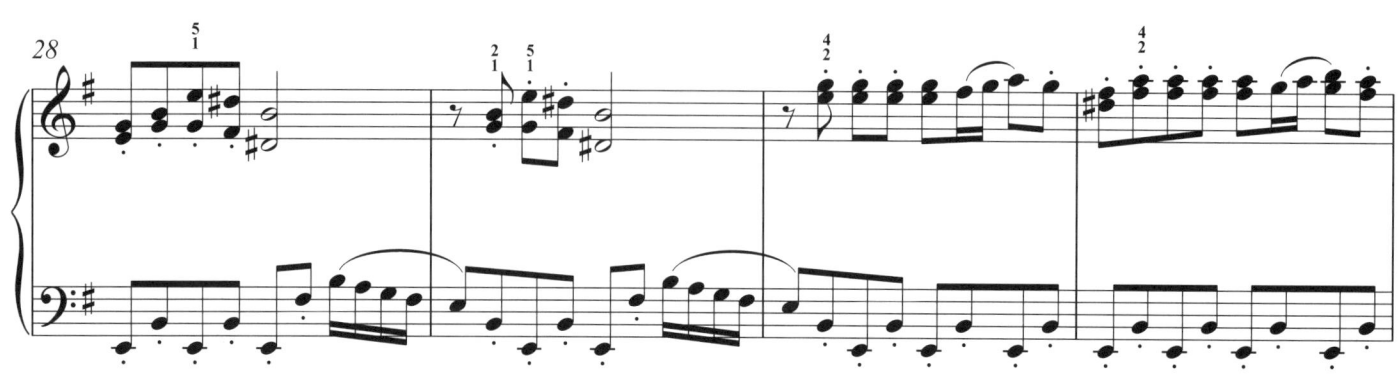
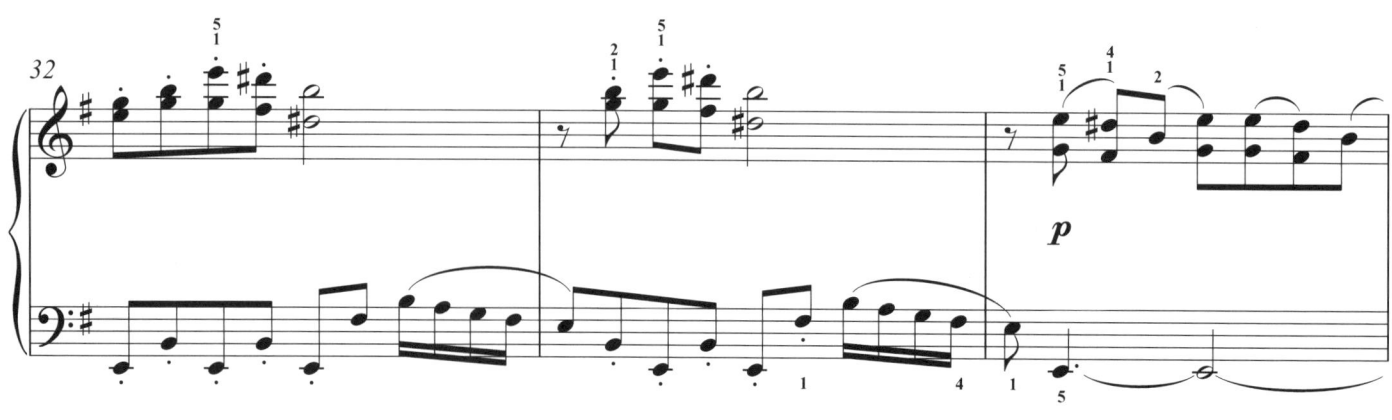

Dance Of The Sugar Plum Fairy
(from 'The Nutcracker Suite', Op.71)

Composed by Pyotr Ilyich Tchaikovsky

© Copyright 2008 Dorsey Brothers Music Limited.
All Rights Reserved. International Copyright Secured.

Dance Of The Reed Flutes (Danse des Mirlitons)
(from 'The Nutcracker Suite', Op.71)

Composed by Pyotr Ilyich Tchaikovsky

© Copyright 2008 Dorsey Brothers Music Limited.
All Rights Reserved. International Copyright Secured.

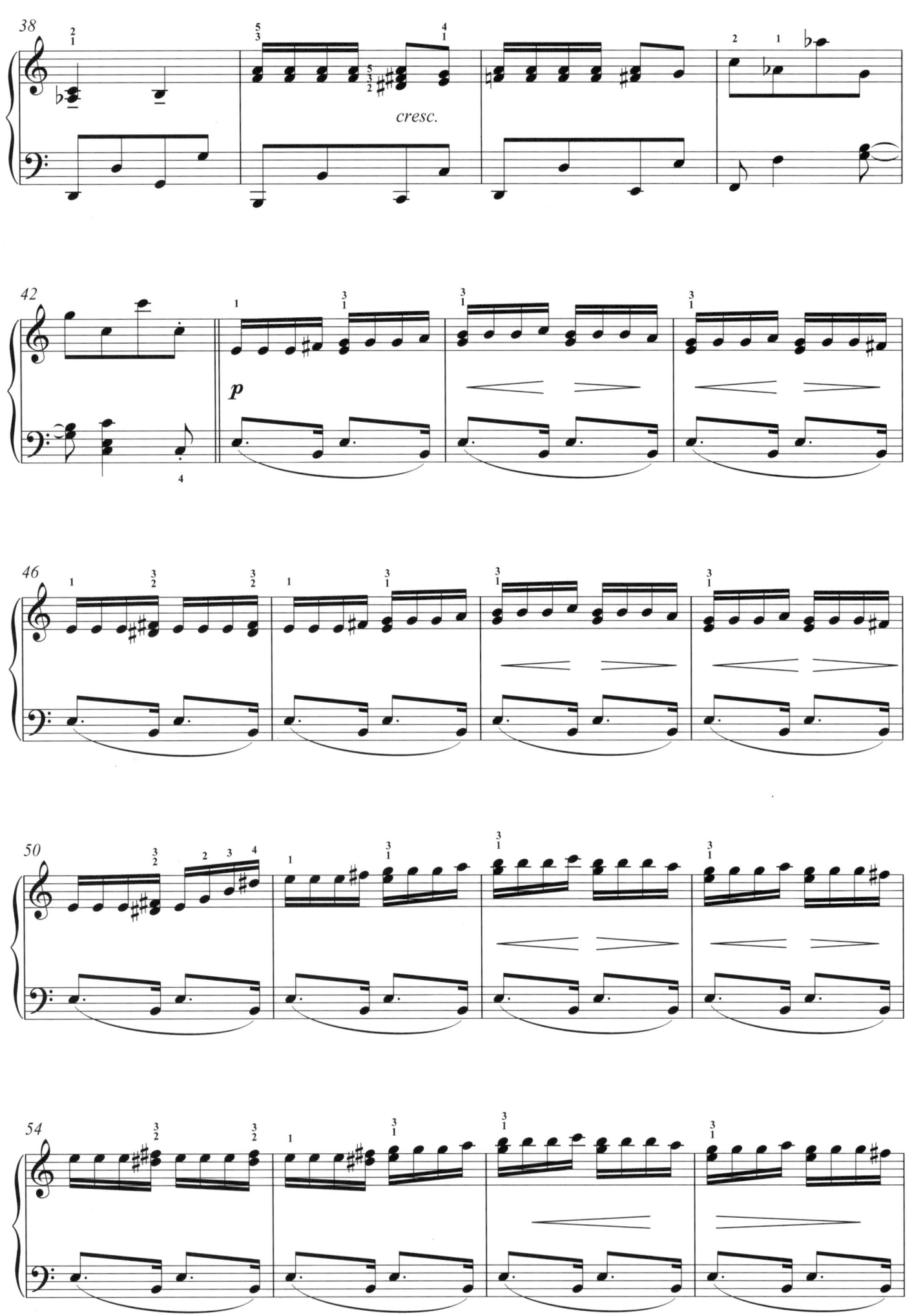

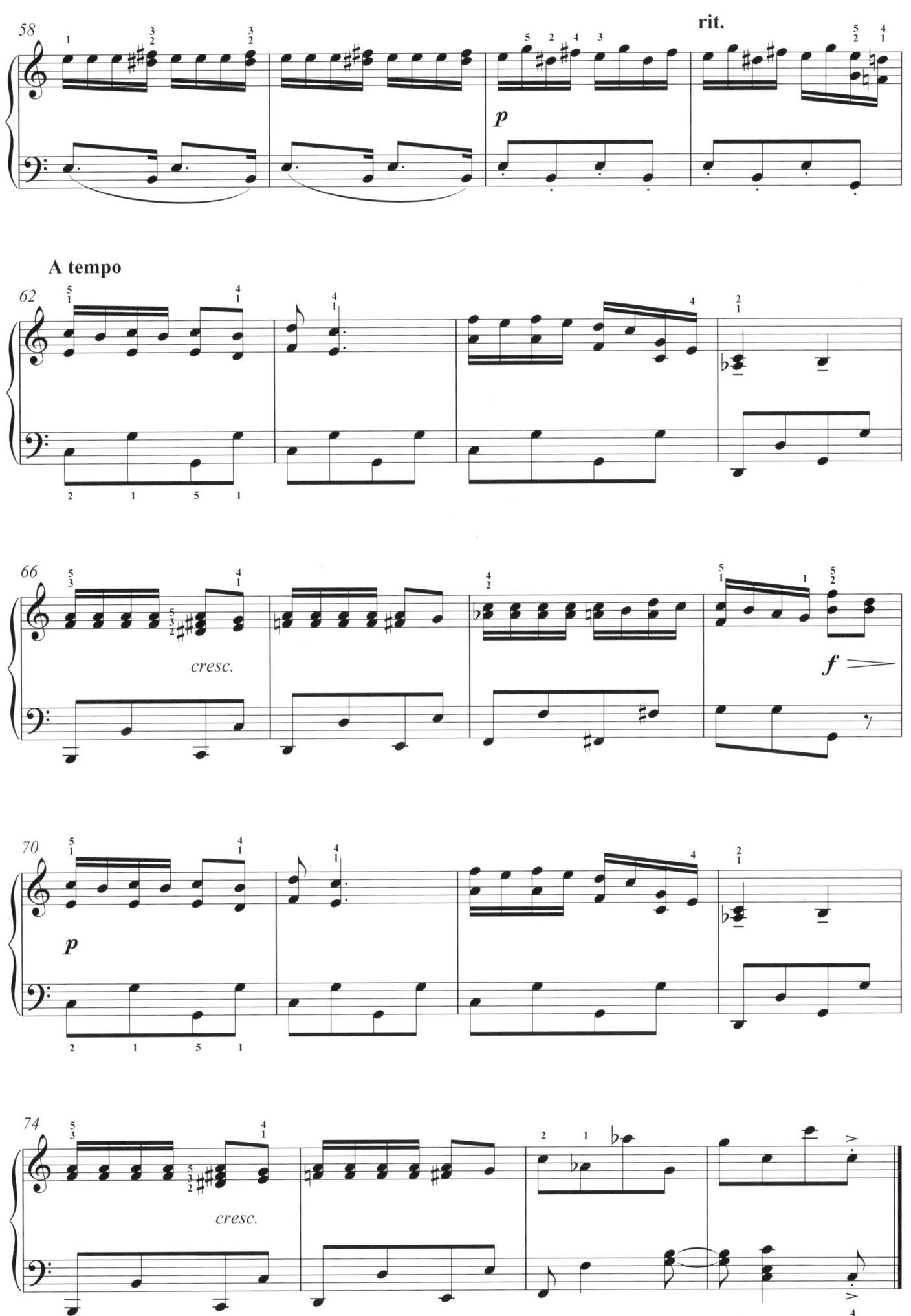

March Of The Wooden Soldiers
(from 'Album For The Young', Op.39, No.5)

Composed by Pyotr Ilyich Tchaikovsky

© Copyright 2008 Dorsey Brothers Music Limited.
All Rights Reserved. International Copyright Secured.

The New Doll
(from 'Album For The Young', Op.39, No.6)

Composed by Pyotr Ilyich Tchaikovsky

This arrangement © Copyright 2003 Chester Music Limited.
All Rights Reserved. International Copyright Secured.

Piano Concerto No.1 in B♭ minor
(Op.23, Opening)

Composed by Pyotr Ilyich Tchaikovsky

© Copyright 2008 Dorsey Brothers Music Limited.
All Rights Reserved. International Copyright Secured.

Allegro non troppo

March from 'The Nutcracker Suite'
(Op.71)

Composed by Pyotr Ilyich Tchaikovsky

© Copyright 2008 Dorsey Brothers Music Limited.
All Rights Reserved. International Copyright Secured.

Tempo di marcia

Prince Gremin's Aria
(from 'Eugene Onegin', Op.24)

Composed by Pyotr Ilyich Tchaikovsky

© Copyright 2008 Dorsey Brothers Music Limited.
All Rights Reserved. International Copyright Secured.

Romeo And Juliet
(Fantasy Overture)

Composed by Pyotr Ilyich Tchaikovsky

© Copyright 2008 Dorsey Brothers Music Limited.
All Rights Reserved. International Copyright Secured.

Allegro giusto

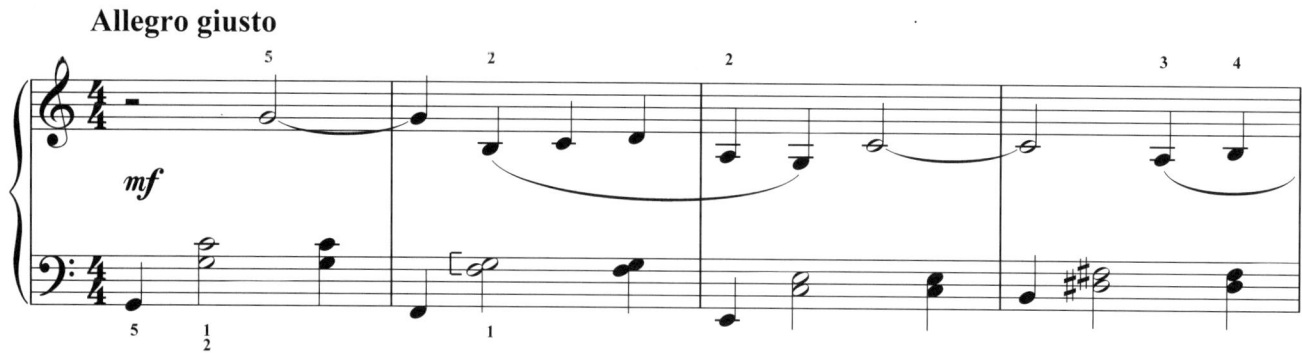

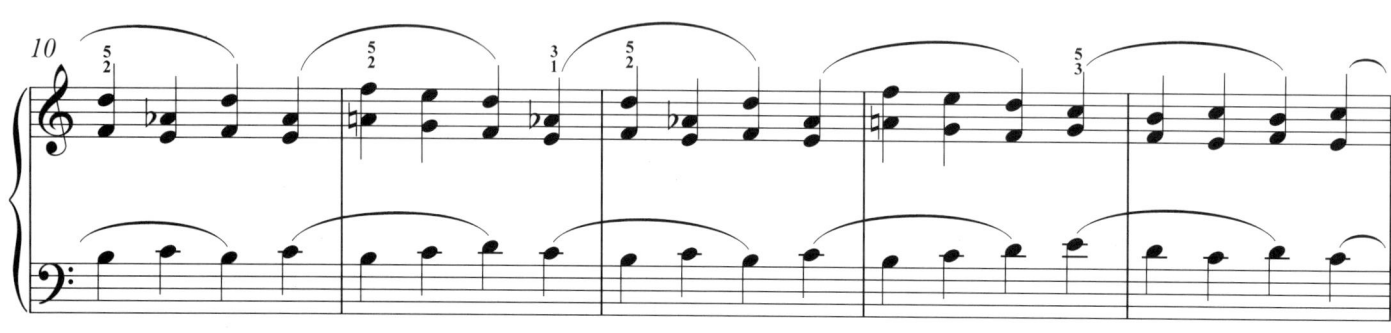

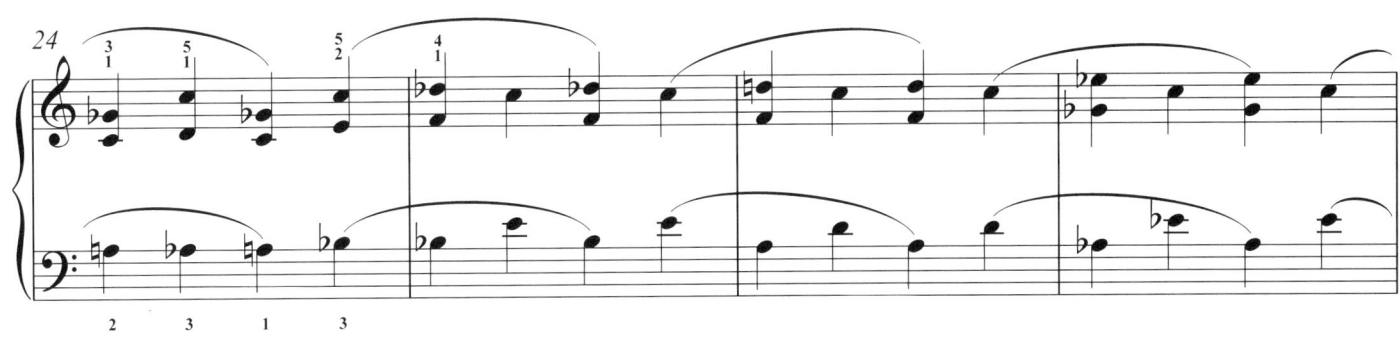
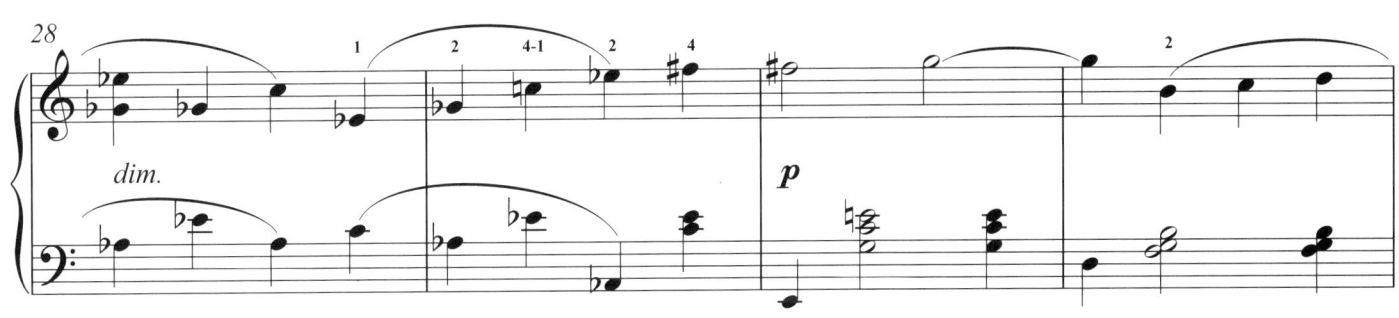

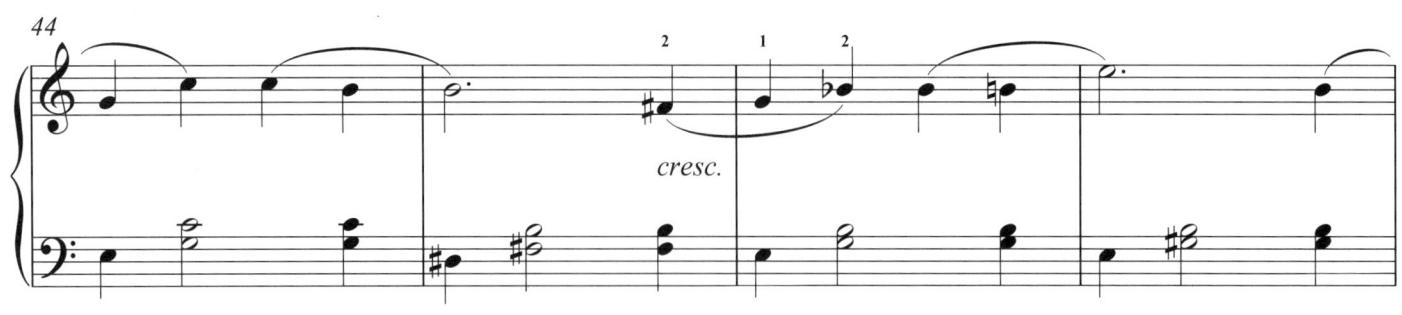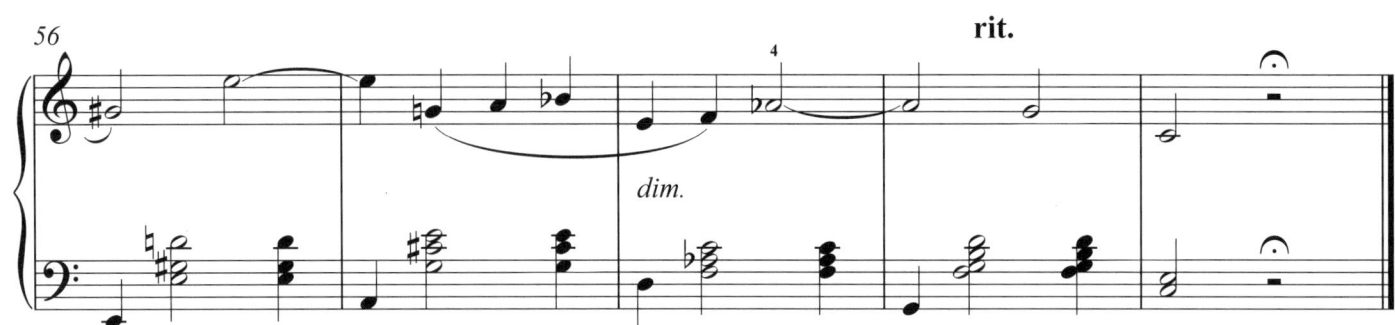

Scene from 'Swan Lake'
(Op.20, No.1)

Composed by Pyotr Ilyich Tchaikovsky

© Copyright 2008 Dorsey Brothers Music Limited.
All Rights Reserved. International Copyright Secured.

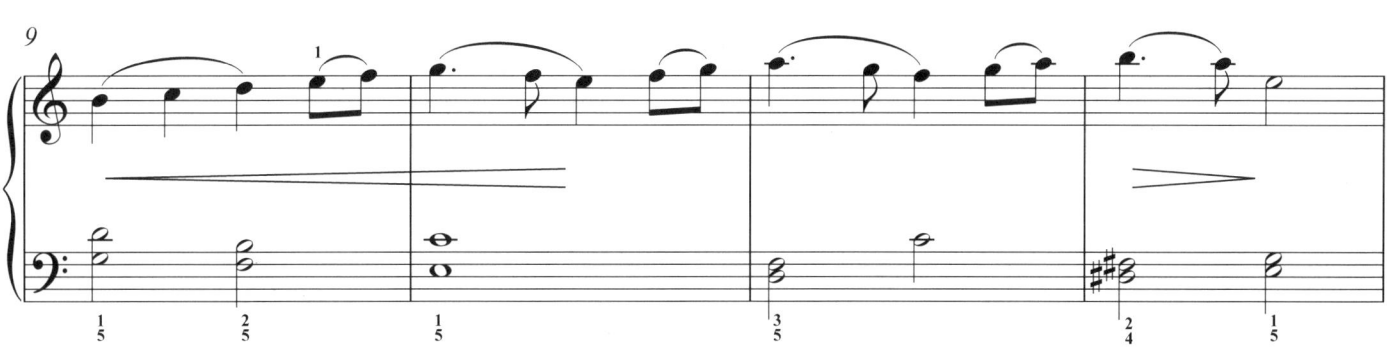

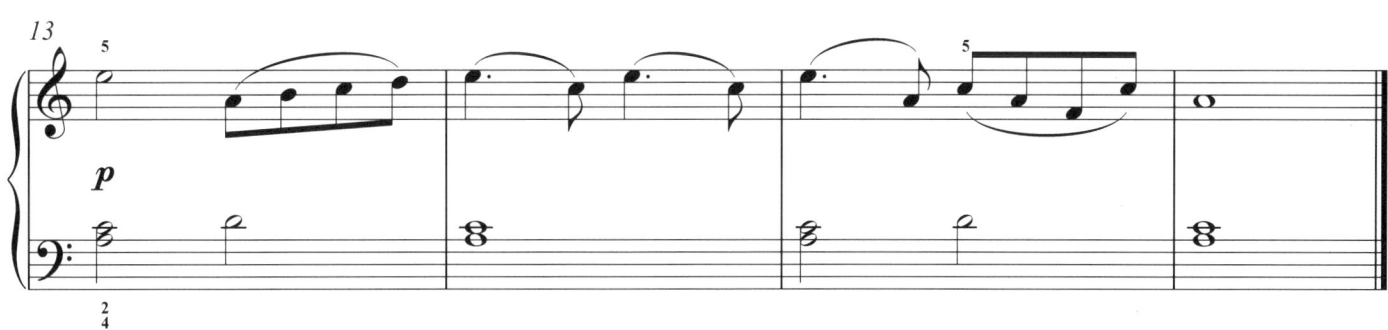

Sentimental Waltz
(from 'Six Pieces', Op.51, No.6)

Composed by Pyotr Ilyich Tchaikovsky

© Copyright 2008 Dorsey Brothers Music Limited.
All Rights Reserved. International Copyright Secured.

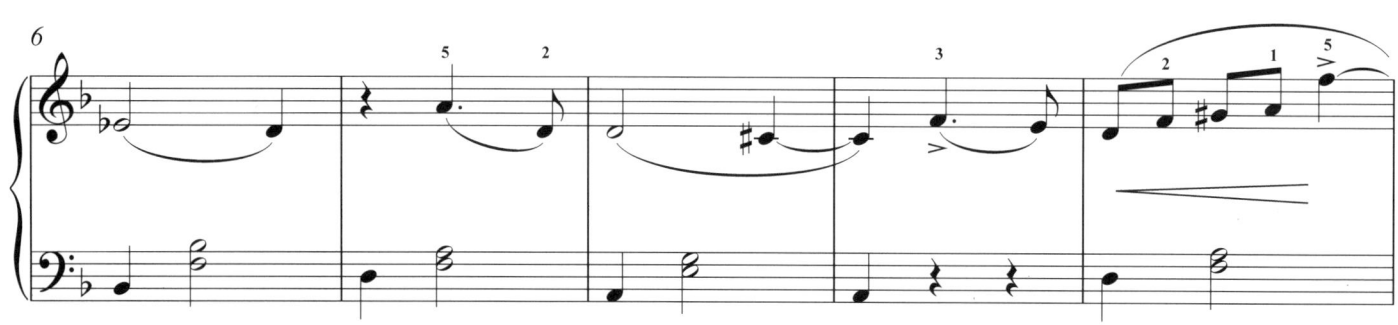

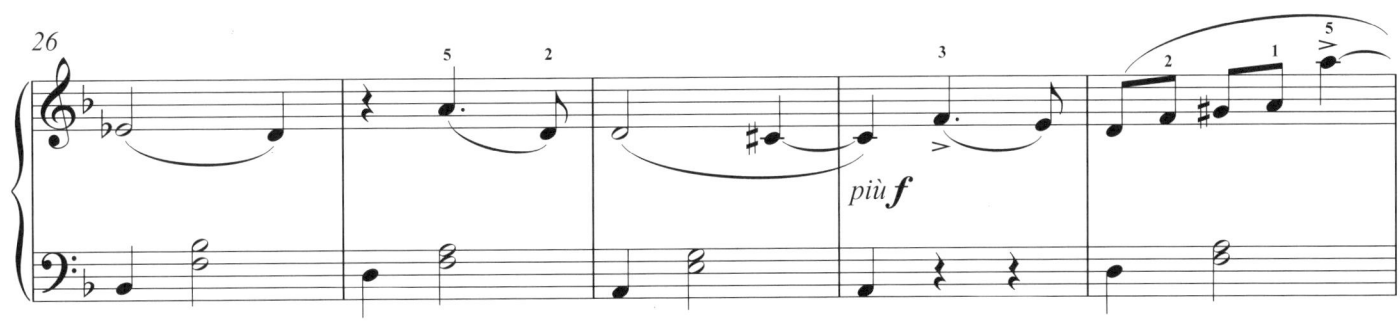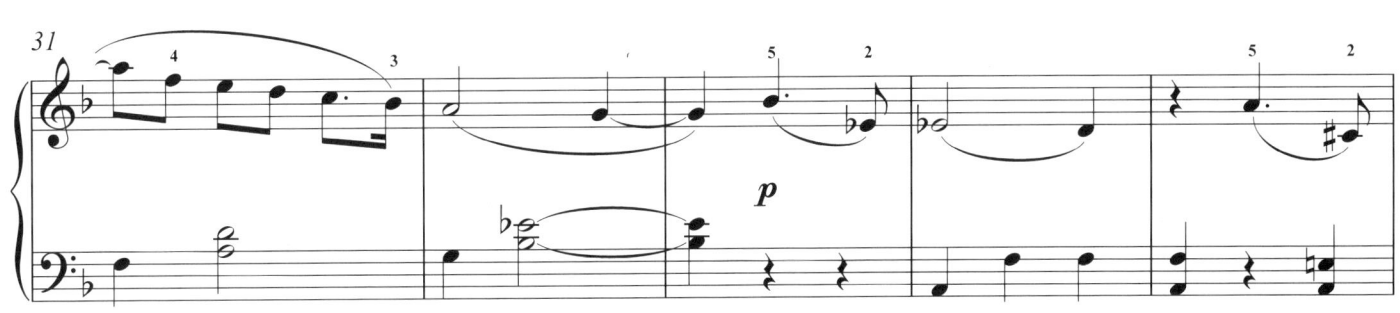

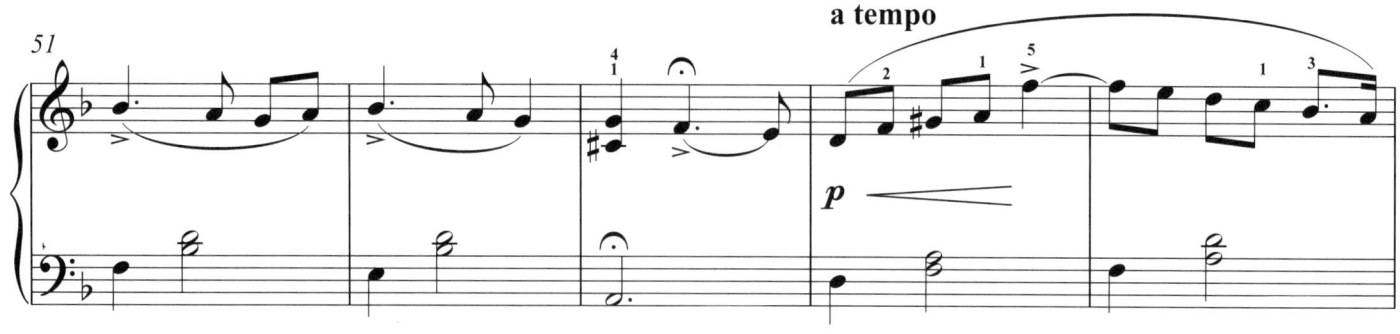

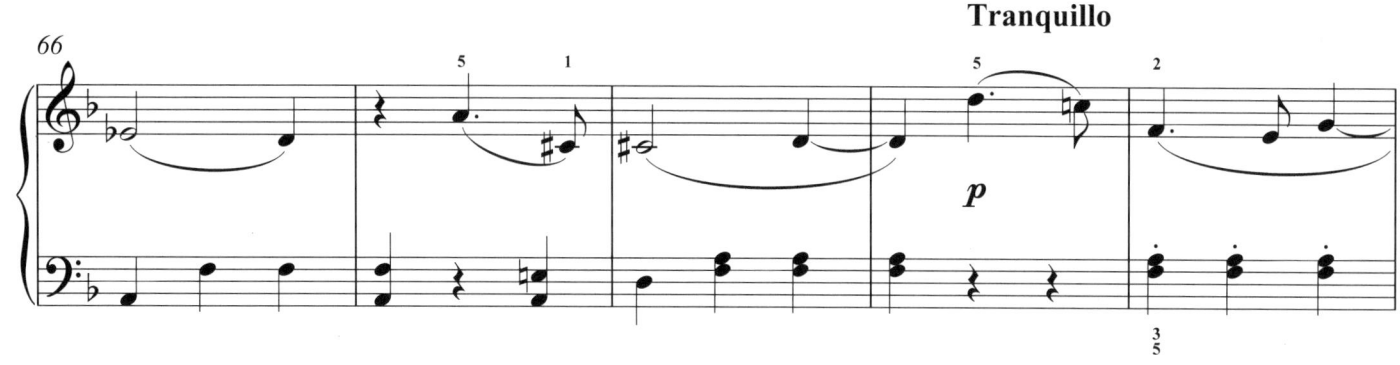

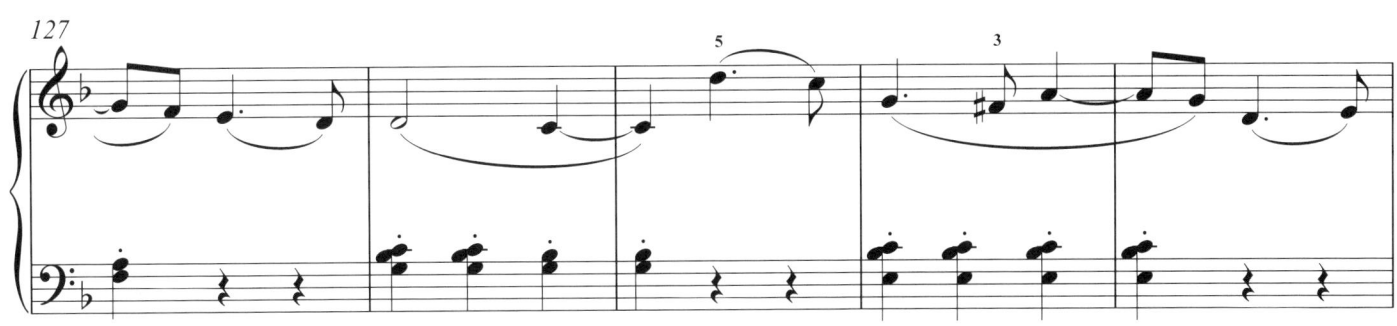

D.S. al Coda ⊕ **Coda**

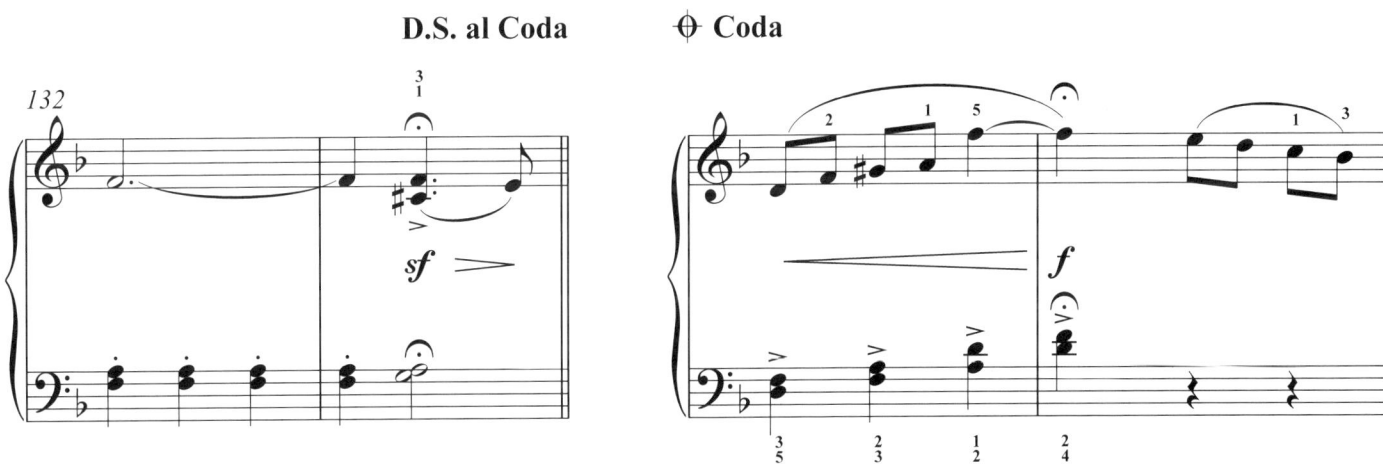

Meno mosso rit.

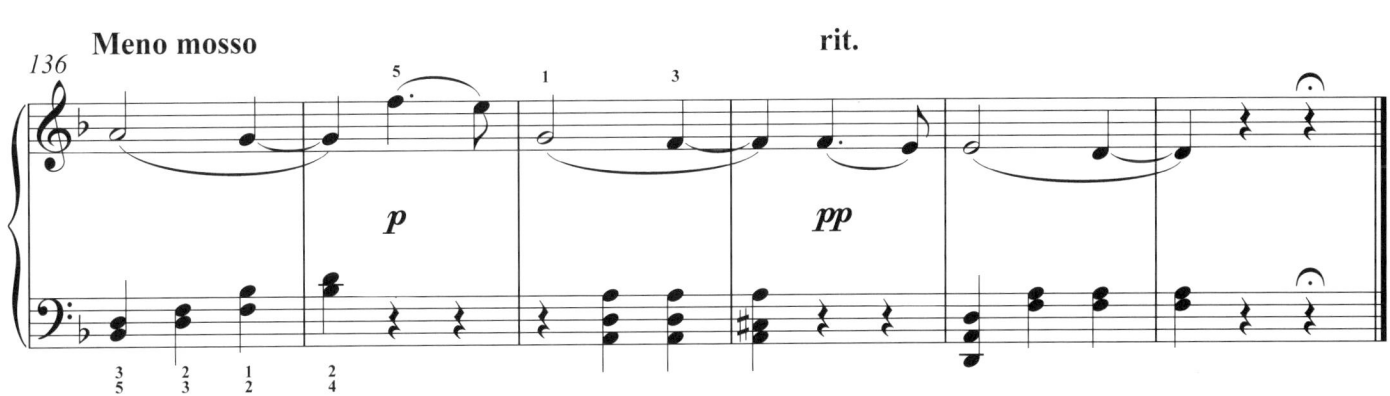

Slavonic March in B♭
(Op.31)

Composed by Pyotr Ilyich Tchaikovsky

© Copyright 2008 Dorsey Brothers Music Limited.
All Rights Reserved. International Copyright Secured.

Allegro moderato

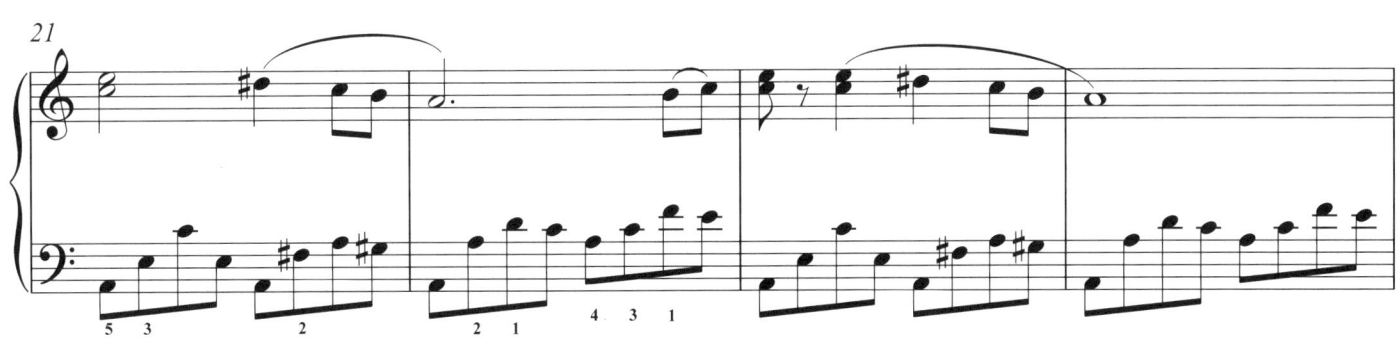

The Sleeping Beauty Waltz
(Op.66, No.5)

Composed by Pyotr Ilyich Tchaikovsky

© Copyright 2008 Dorsey Brothers Music Limited.
All Rights Reserved. International Copyright Secured.

Allegro (Tempo di valse)

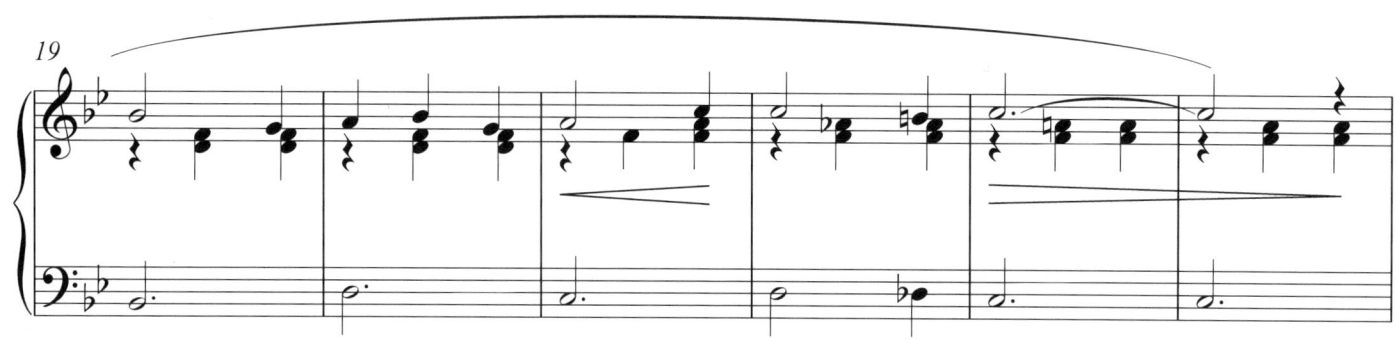

Symphony No.6 'Pathétique', Op.74
(1st Movement)

Composed by Pyotr Ilyich Tchaikovsky

© Copyright 2008 Dorsey Brothers Music Limited.
All Rights Reserved. International Copyright Secured.

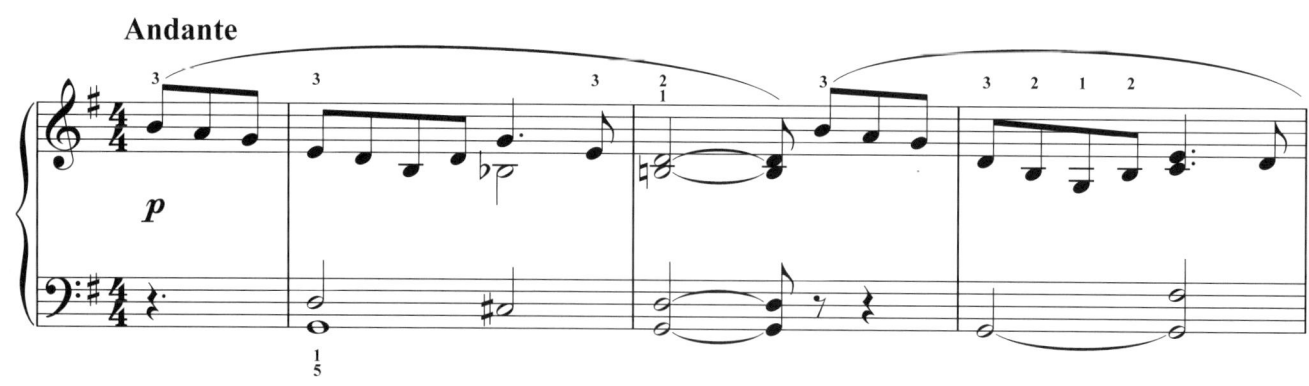

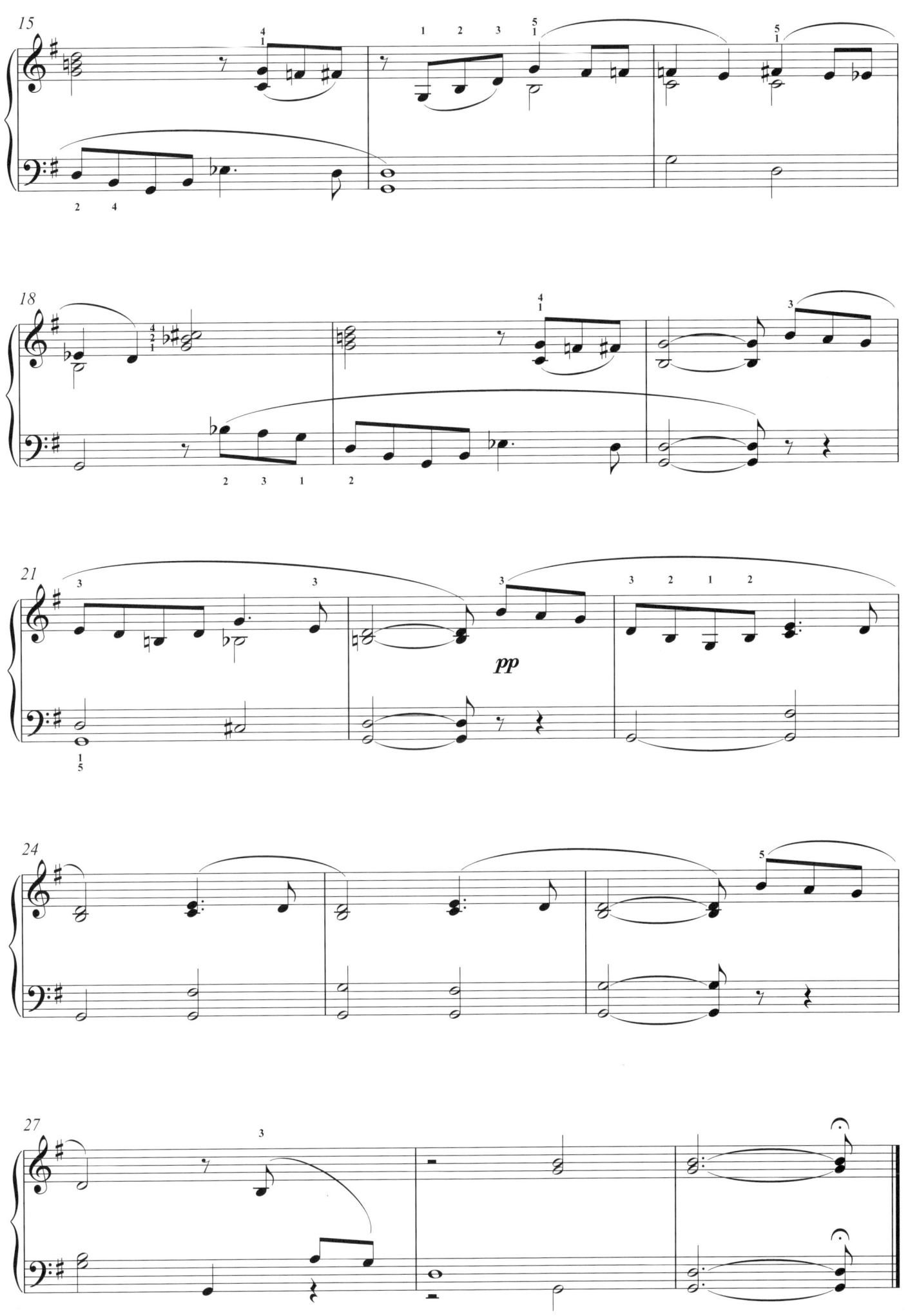

Symphony No.6 'Pathétique', Op.74
(3rd Movement March)

Composed by Pyotr Ilyich Tchaikovsky

© Copyright 2008 Dorsey Brothers Music Limited.
All Rights Reserved. International Copyright Secured.

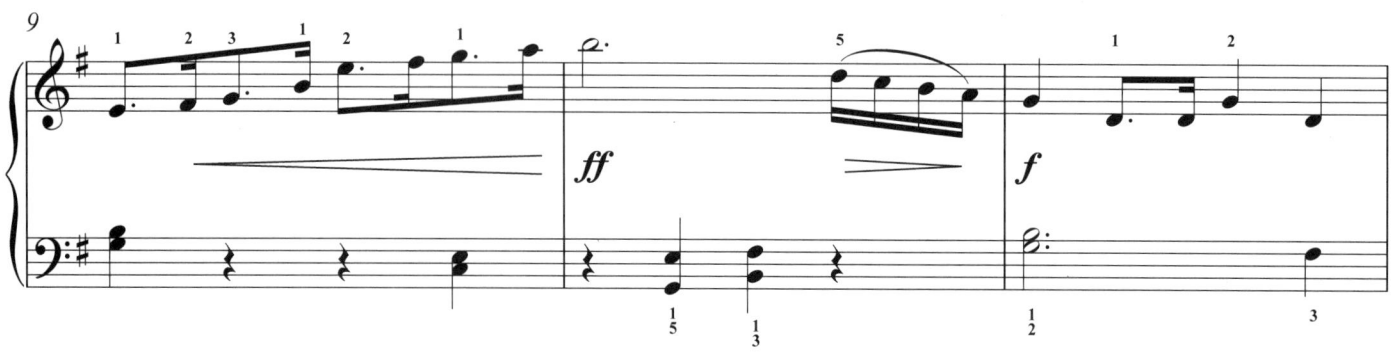

46

Symphony No.5 in E minor, Op.64
(Andante Cantabile Theme)

Composed by Pyotr Ilyich Tchaikovsky

© Copyright 2008 Dorsey Brothers Music Limited.
All Rights Reserved. International Copyright Secured.

Waltz from 'Serenade For Strings'
(Op.48)

Composed by Pyotr Ilyich Tchaikovsky

© Copyright 2008 Dorsey Brothers Music Limited.
All Rights Reserved. International Copyright Secured.

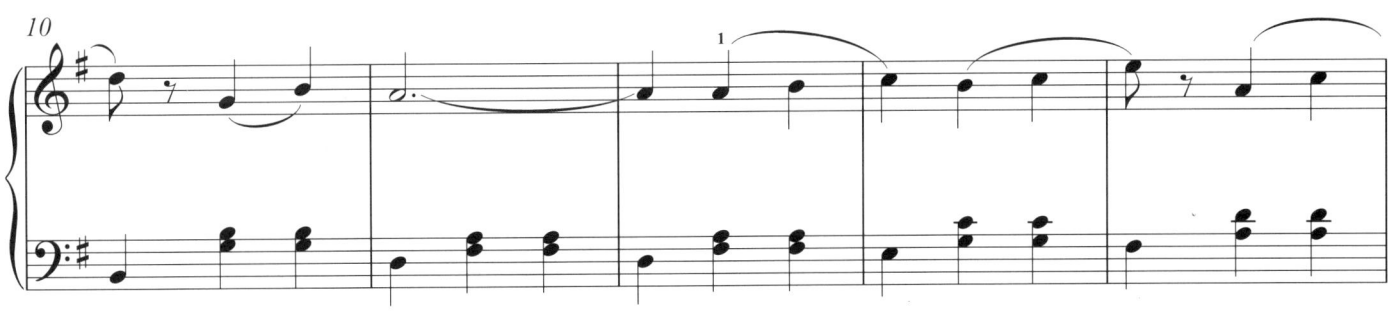

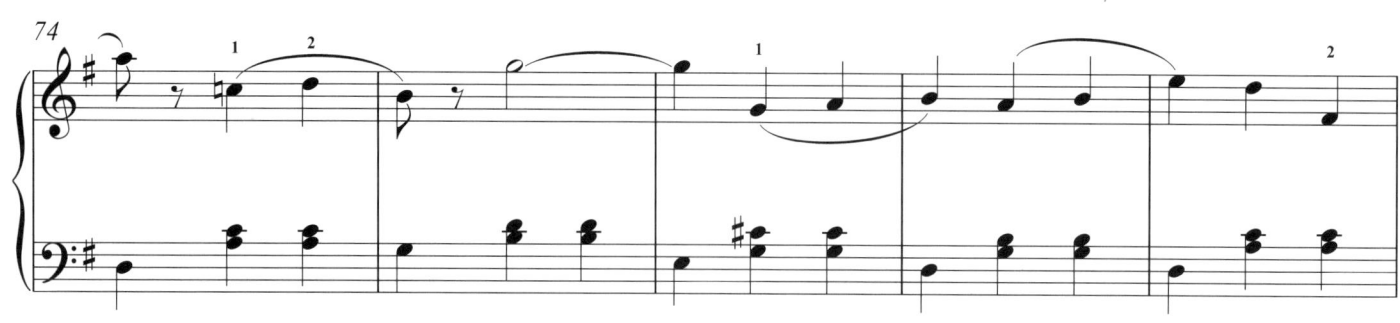
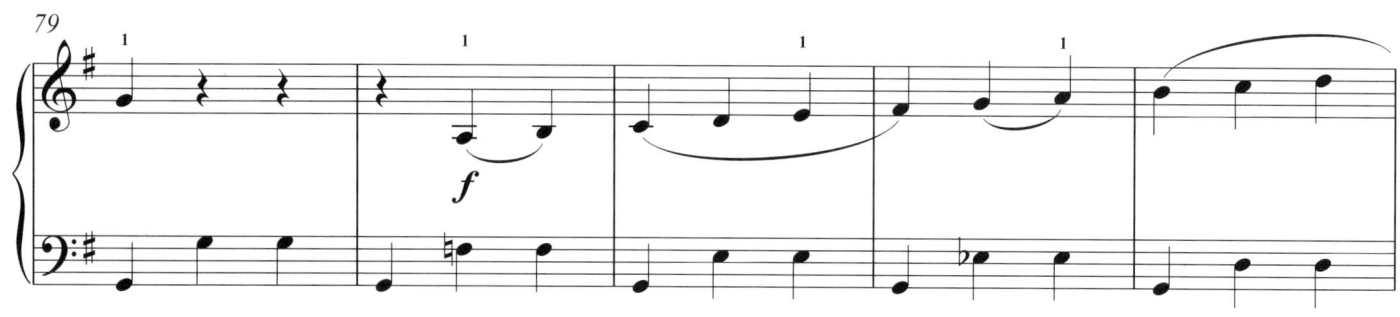
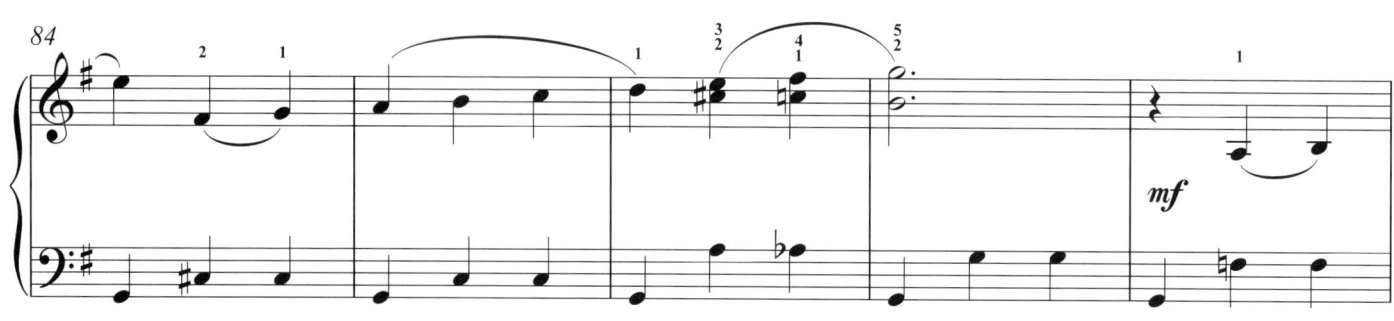

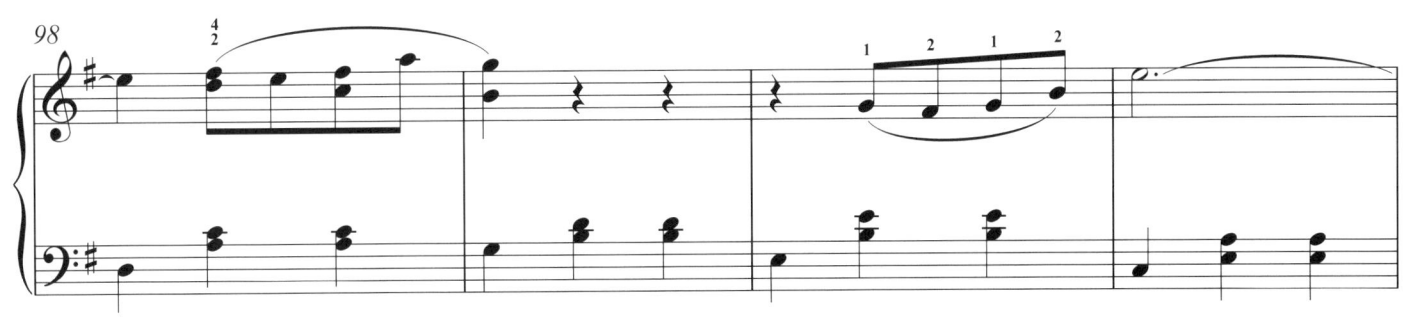
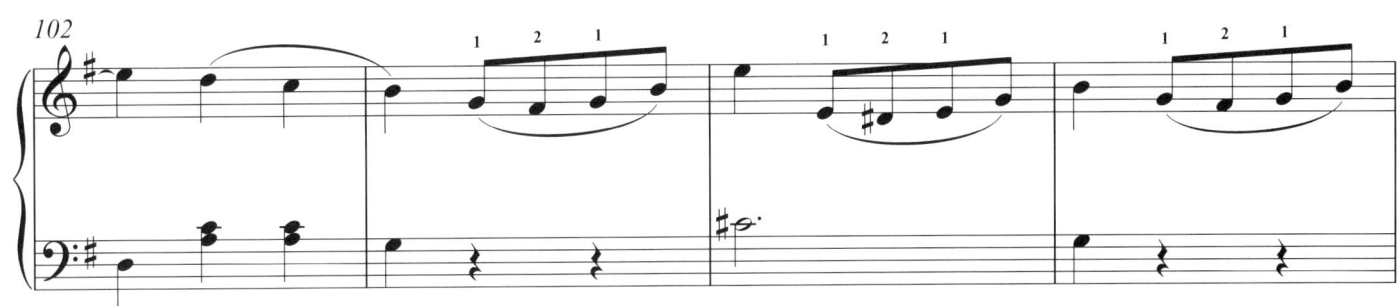
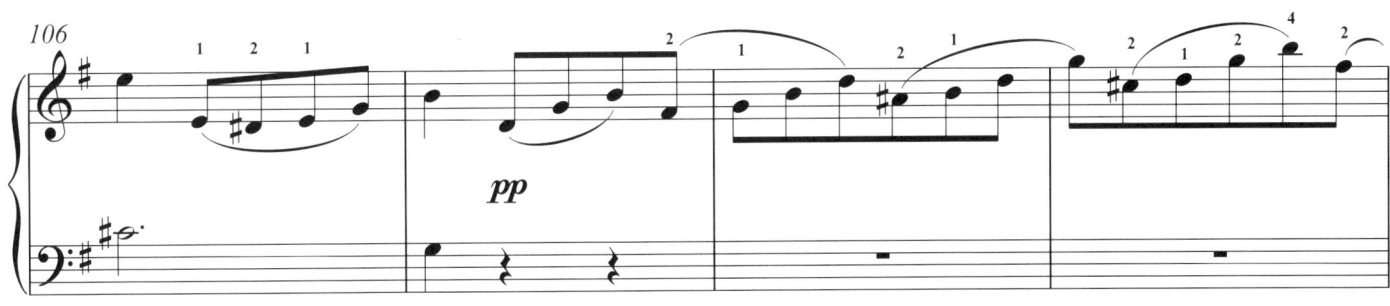

Waltz in E♭ major
(from 'Album For The Young', Op.39, No.9)

Composed by Pyotr Ilyich Tchaikovsky

© Copyright 2008 Dorsey Brothers Music Limited.
All Rights Reserved. International Copyright Secured.

Waltz Of The Flowers
(from 'The Nutcracker Suite', Op.71)

Composed by Pyotr Ilyich Tchaikovsky

© Copyright 2008 Dorsey Brothers Music Limited.
All Rights Reserved. International Copyright Secured.

Tempo di valse moderato

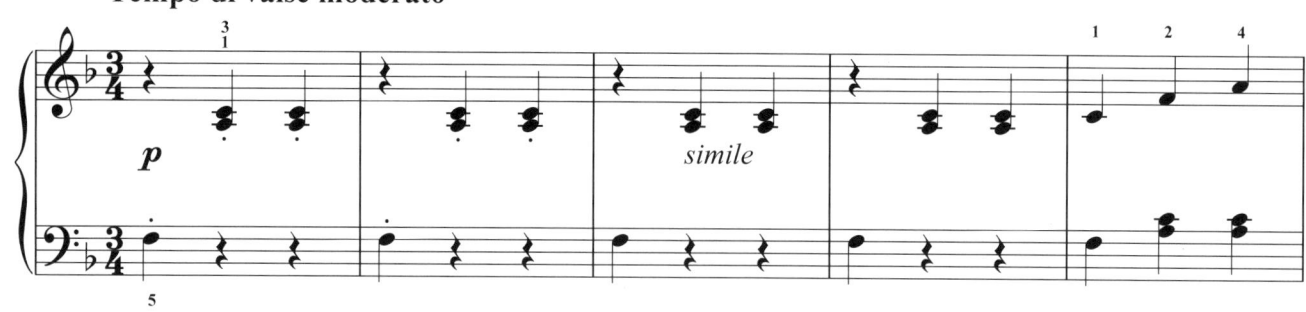

56

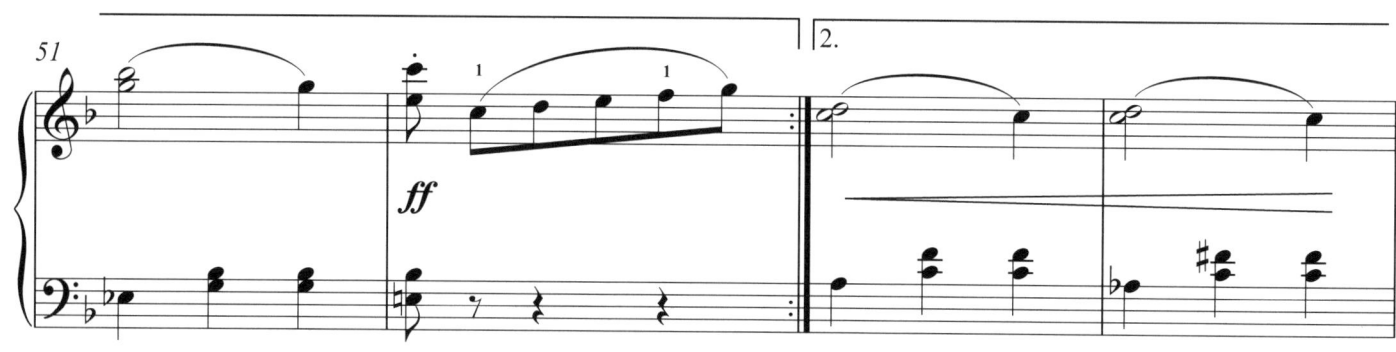

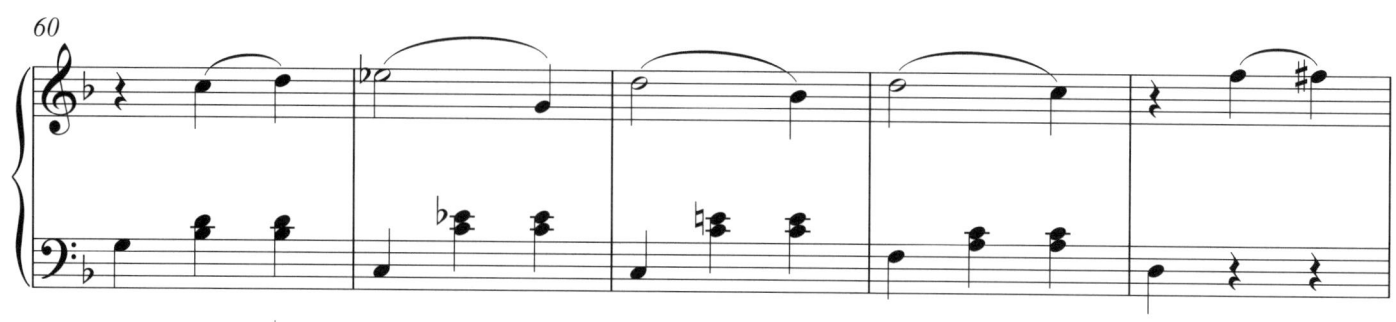

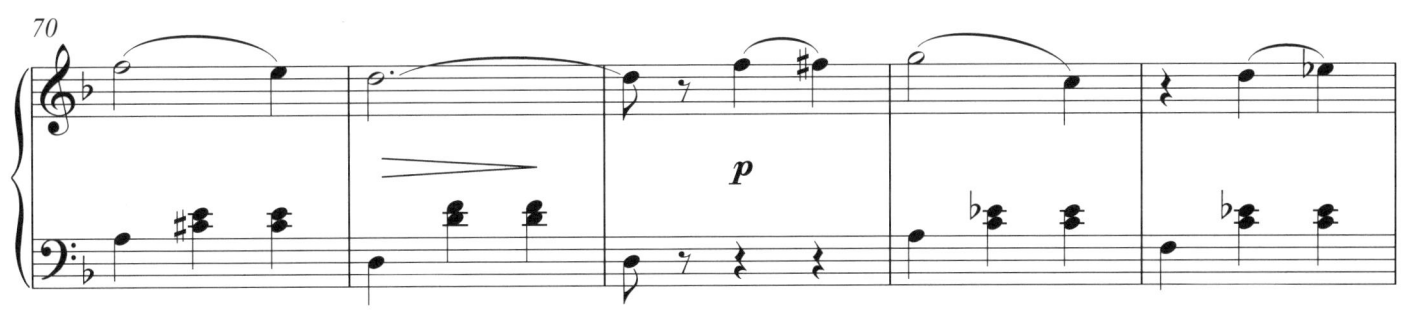
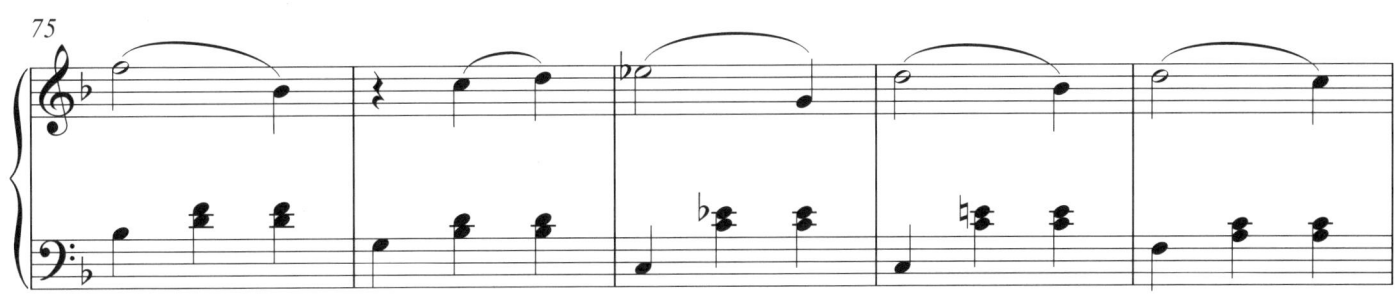

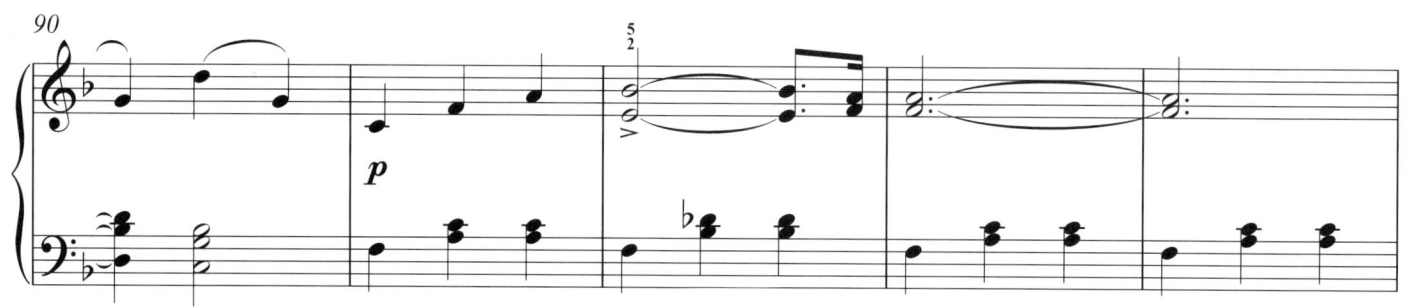

Waltz from 'Swan Lake'
(Op.20, No.2)

Composed by Pyotr Ilyich Tchaikovsky

© Copyright 2008 Dorsey Brothers Music Limited.
All Rights Reserved. International Copyright Secured.

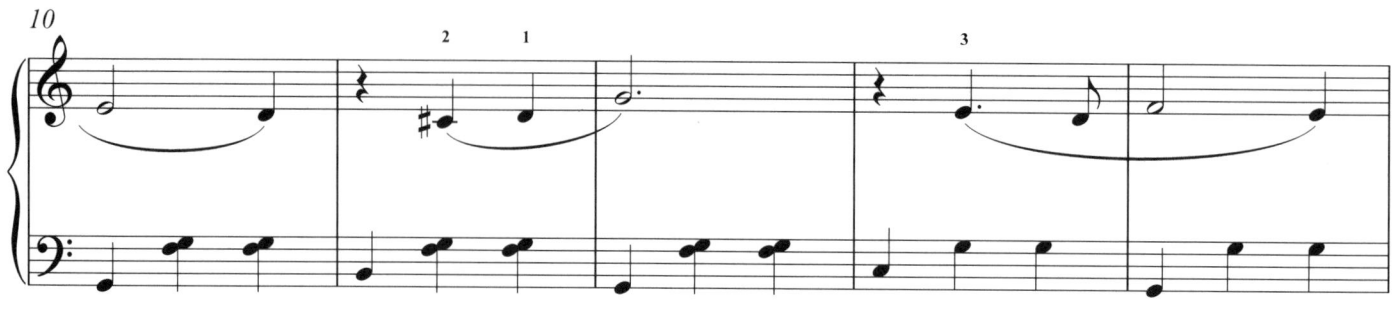

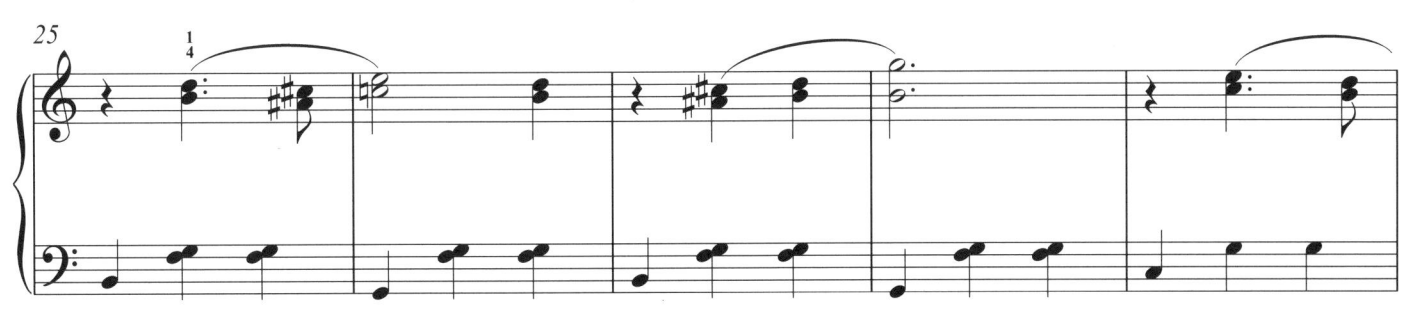